The Verse-Book Of A Homely Woman

Elizabeth Rebecca Ward,

AKA Fay Inchfawn

Contents

PART I. INDOORS 7
The Long View 7
Within my House 8
The Housewife 10
To Mother 11
In Such an Hour 13
The Daily Interview 14
The Little House 17
The House-Mother 19
A Woman in Hospital 20
In Convalescence 24
Homesick 26
On Washing Day 28
When Baby Strayed 29
If Only ---- 31
Listening 33
The Dear Folks in Devon 34
The Reason 35
Two Women 36
The Prize Fight 38
The Home Lights 40
To an Old Teapot 42
To a Rebellious Daughter 43
For Mothering! 46
Little Fan 47
The Naughty Day 48
To a Little White Bird 49
Because 50
When He Comes 51
PART II. OUT OF DOORS 53
Early Spring 53
The Witness 54
In Somerset 55
Song of a Woodland Stream 55
    Luggage in Advance 57
At the Cross Roads 58
Summer met Me 59
The Carrier 60
The Lad's Love by the Gate 61
The Thrush 62
In Dorset Dear 63

The Flight of the Fairies	64
The Street Player	65
On All Souls' Eve	67
The Log Fire	69
God save the King	70

THE VERSE-BOOK
OF A HOMELY WOMAN

BY

Elizabeth Rebecca Ward,
AKA Fay Inchfawn

PART I. INDOORS

The Long View

Some day of days! Some dawning
   yet to be
I shall be clothed with immortality!

And, in that day, I shall not greatly care
That Jane spilt candle grease upon the
   stair.

It will not grieve me then, as once it did,
That careless hands have chipped my
   teapot lid.

I groan, being burdened. But, in that
   glad day,
I shall forget vexations of the way.

That needs were often great, when means
   were small,
Will not perplex me any more at all
A few short years at most (it may be less),

I shall have done with earthly storm and
  stress.

So, for this day, I lay me at Thy feet.
O, keep me sweet, my Master! Keep
  me sweet!

Within my House

First, there's the entrance, narrow,
  and so small,
The hat-stand seems to fill the tiny hall;
That staircase, too, has such an awkward
  bend,
The carpet rucks, and rises up on end!
Then, all the rooms are cramped and close
  together;
And there's a musty smell in rainy weather.
Yes, and it makes the daily work go hard
To have the only tap across a yard.
These creaking doors, these draughts, this
  battered paint,
Would try, I think, the temper of a saint,

How often had I railed against these
  things,
With envies, and with bitter murmurings
For spacious rooms, and sunny garden
  plots!

Until one day,
Washing the breakfast dishes, so I think,
I paused a moment in my work to pray;
And then and there
All life seemed suddenly made new and
   fair;
For, like the Psalmist's dove among the
   pots
(Those endless pots, that filled the tiny
   sink!),
My spirit found her wings.

"Lord" (thus I prayed), "it matters not
   at all
That my poor home is ill-arranged and
   small:
I, not the house, am straitened; Lord,
   'tis I!
Enlarge my foolish heart, that by-and-by
I may look up with such a radiant face
Thou shalt have glory even in this place.
And when I trip, or stumble unawares
In carrying water up these awkward stairs,
Then keep me sweet, and teach me day
   by day
To tread with patience Thy appointed
   way.
As for the house . . . . Lord, let it be
   my part
To walk within it with a perfect heart."

The Housewife

See, I am cumbered, Lord,
  With serving, and with small vexa-
    tious things.
Upstairs, and down, my feet
Must hasten, sure and fleet.
So weary that I cannot heed Thy word;
So tired, I cannot now mount up with
    wings.
I wrestle--how I wrestle!--through the
    hours.
Nay, not with principalities, nor powers--
Dark spiritual foes of God's and man's--
But with antagonistic pots and pans:
With footmarks in the hall,
With smears upon the wall,
With doubtful ears, and small unwashen
    hands,
And with a babe's innumerable demands.

I toil with feverish haste, while tear-drops
    glisten,

(O, child of mine, be still. And listen--
    listen!)

At last, I laid aside
Important work, no other hands could do
So well (I thought), no skill contrive so
    true.
And with my heart's door open--open

wide--
With leisured feet, and idle hands, I sat.
I, foolish, fussy, blind as any bat,
Sat down to listen, and to learn. And lo,
My thousand tasks were done the better so.

To Mother

I would that you should know,
Dear mother, that I love you--love
   you so!
That I remember other days and years;
Remember childish joys and childish fears.
And this, because my baby's little hand
Opened my own heart's door and made
   me understand.

I wonder how you could
Be always kind and good!
So quick to hear; to tend
My smallest ills; to lend
Such sympathising ears
Swifter than ancient seer's.
I never yet knew hands so soft and kind,
Nor any cheek so smooth, nor any mind
So full of tender thoughts. . . . Dear
   mother, now
I think that I can guess a little how
You must have looked for some response,

some sign,
That all my tiresome wayward heart was
   thine.

And sure it was! You were my first dear
   love!
You who first pointed me to God above;
You who seemed hearkening to my lightest
   word,
And in the dark night seasons always
   heard
When I came trembling, knocking at your
   door.
Forgive me, mother, if my whims outwore
Your patient heart. Or if in later days
I sought out foolish unfamiliar ways;
If ever, mother dear, I loosed my hold
Of your loved hand; or, headstrong,
   thought you cold,
Forgive me, mother! Oh, forgive me,
   dear!
I am come back at last--you see me
   here,
Your loving child. . . . And, mother,
   on my knee
I pray that thus my child may think of
   me!

In Such an Hour

Sometimes, when everything goes
   wrong:
When days are short, and nights are long;
When wash-day brings so dull a sky
That not a single thing will dry.
And when the kitchen chimney smokes,
And when there's naught so "queer" as
   folks!
When friends deplore my faded youth,
And when the baby cuts a tooth.
While John, the baby last but one,
Clings round my skirts till day is done;
When fat, good-tempered Jane is glum,
And butcher's man forgets to come.

Sometimes, I say, on days like these,
I get a sudden gleam of bliss.
"Not on some sunny day of ease,
He'll come .. but on a day like this!"
And, in the twinkling of an eye,
These tiresome things will all go by!

And, 'tis a curious thing, but Jane
Is sure, just then, to smile again;
Or, out the truant sun will peep,
And both the babies fall asleep.
The fire burns up with roar sublime,
And butcher's man is just in time.
And oh! My feeble faith grows strong
Sometimes, when everything goes wrong!

The Daily Interview

Such a sensation Sunday's preacher
   made.
"Christian!" he cried, "what is your stock-
   in-trade?
Alas! Too often nil. No time to pray;
No interview with Christ from day to day,
A hurried prayer, maybe, just gabbled
   through;
A random text--for any one will do."
Then gently, lovingly, with look intense,
He leaned towards us--
"Is this common sense?
No person in his rightful mind will try
To run his business so, lest by-and-by
The thing collapses, smirching his good
   name,
And he, insolvent, face the world with
shame."

I heard it all; and something inly said
That all was true. The daily toil and press
Had crowded out my hopes of holiness.
Still, my old self rose, reasoning:
How can you,
With strenuous work to do--
Real slogging work--say, how can you
   keep pace
With leisured folks? Why, you could
   grow in grace
If you had time . . . the daily Interview

Was never meant for those who wash and
 bake.

But yet a small Voice whispered:
"For My sake
Keep tryst with Me!
There are so many minutes in a day,
So spare Me ten.
It shall be proven, then,
Ten minutes set apart can well repay
You shall accomplish more
If you will shut your door
For ten short minutes just to watch and
 pray."

"Lord, if I do
Set ten apart for You"
(I dared, yes dared, to reason thus with
 Him)
"The baker's sure to come;
Or Jane will call
To say some visitor is in the hall;
Or I shall smell the porridge burning, yes,
And run to stop it in my hastiness.
There's not ten minutes, Lord, in all the
 day
I can be sure of peace in which to watch
 and pray."

But all that night,
With calm insistent might,
That gentle Voice spake softly, lovingly--
"Keep tryst with Me!

You have devised a dozen different ways
Of getting easy meals on washing days;
You spend much anxious thought on
    hopeless socks;
On moving ironmould from tiny frocks;
'Twas you who found
A way to make the sugar lumps go round;
You, who invented ways and means of
    making
Nice spicy buns for tea, hot from the baking,
When margarine was short . . . and can-
    not you
Who made the time to join the butter queue
Make time again for Me?
Yes, will you not, with all your daily
    striving,
Use woman's wit in scheming and con-
    triving
To keep that tryst with Me?"

Like ice long bound
On powdered frosty ground,
My erring will all suddenly gave way.
The kind soft wind of His sweet pleading
    blew,
And swiftly, silently, before I knew,
The warm love loosed and ran.
Life-giving floods began,
And so most lovingly I answered Him:
"Lord, yes, I will, and can.
I will keep tryst with Thee, Lord, come
    what may!"

ENVOY.

It is a wondrous and surprising thing
How that ten minutes takes the piercing
 sting
From vexing circumstance and poison-
 ous dart
Hurled by the enemy straight at my
 heart.
So, to the woman tempest-tossed and
 tried
By household cares, and hosts of things
 beside,
With all my strength God bids me say
 to you:
"Dear soul, do try the daily Interview!"

The Little House

One yestereve, in the waning light,
When the wind was still and the
 gloaming bright,
There came a breath from a far countrie,
And the ghost of a Little House called
 to me.

"Have you forgotten me?" "No!" I cried.
"Your hall was as narrow as this is wide,
Your roof was leaky, the rain came

    through
Till a ceiling fell, on my new frock too!

"In your parlour flooring a loose board hid,
And wore the carpet, you know it did!
Your kitchen was small, and the shelves
    were few,
While the fireplace smoked--and you
    know it's true!"

The little ghost sighed: "Do you quite
    forget
My window boxes of mignonette?
And the sunny room where you used to
    sew
When a great hope came to you, long ago?

"Ah, me! How you used to watch the
    door
Where a latch-key turned on the stroke
    of four.
And you made the tea, and you poured
    it out
From an old brown pot with a broken
    spout

"Now, times have changed. And your
    footman waits
With the silver urn, and the fluted plates.
But the little blind Love with the wings,
    has flown,
Who used to sit by your warm hearth-
    stone."

The little ghost paused. Then "Away!"
   I said.
"Back to your place with the quiet dead.
Back to your place, lest my servants see,
That the ghost of a Little House calls
   to me."

The House-Mother

Across the town the evening bell is
   ringing;
Clear comes the call, through kitchen
   windows winging!

Lord, knowing Thou art kind,
I heed Thy call to prayer.
I have a soul to save;
A heart which needs, I think, a double
   share
Of sweetnesses which noble ladies crave.
Hope, faith and diligence, and patient
   care,
With meekness, grace, and lowliness of
   mind.
Lord, wilt Thou grant all these
To one who prays, but cannot sit at ease?

They do not know,
The passers-by, who go

Up to Thy house, with saintly faces set;
Who throng about Thy seat,
And sing Thy praises sweet,
Till vials full of odours cloud Thy feet;
They do not know . . .
And, if they knew, then would they greatly care
That Thy tired handmaid washed the children's hair;
Or, with red roughened hands, scoured dishes well,
While through the window called the evening bell?
And that her seeking soul looks upward yet,
THEY do not know . . . but THOU wilt not forget

A Woman in Hospital

I know it all . . . I know.
For I am God. I am Jehovah, He
Who made you what you are; and I can see
The tears that wet your pillow night by night,
When nurse has lowered that too-brilliant light;
When the talk ceases, and the ward grows

still,
And you have doffed your will:
I know the anguish and the helplessness.
I know the fears that toss you to and fro.
And how you wrestle, weariful,
With hosts of little strings that pull
About your heart, and tear it so.
I know.

Lord, do You know
I had no time to put clean curtains up;
No time to finish darning all the socks;
Nor sew clean frilling in the children's
   frocks?
And do You know about my Baby's cold?
And how things are with my sweet three-
   year-old?
Will Jane remember right
Their cough mixture at night?
And will she ever think
To brush the kitchen flues, or scrub the
   sink?

And then, there's John! Poor tired
   lonely John!
No one will run to put his slippers on.
And not a soul but me
Knows just exactly how he likes his tea.
It rends my heart to think I cannot go
And minister to him. . . .

I know. I know.

Then, there are other things,
Dear Lord . . . more little strings
That pull my heart. Now Baby feels her
   feet
She loves to run outside into the street
And Jane's hands are so full, she'll never
   see. . . .
And I'm quite sure the clean clothes won't
   be aired--
At least, not properly.
And, oh, I can't, I really can't be spared--
My little house calls so!

I know.
And I am waiting here to help and bless.
Lay down your head. Lay down your hope-
   lessness
And let Me speak.
You are so weary, child, you are so weak.
But let us reason out
The darkness and the doubt;
This torturing fear that tosses you about.

I hold the universe. I count the stars.
And out of shortened lives I build the
   ages. . . .

But, Lord, while such high things Thy
   thought engages,
I fear--forgive me--lest
Amid those limitless eternal spaces
Thou shouldest, in the high and heavenly
   places,

Pass over my affairs as things of nought.
There are so many houses just like mine.
And I so earth-bound, and Thyself Divine.
It seems impossible that Thou shouldst
   care
Just what my babies wear;
And what John gets to eat; . . . and
   can it be
A circumstance of great concern to Thee
Whether I live or die?

Have you forgotten then, My child, that I,
The Infinite, the Limitless, laid down
The method of existence that I knew,
And took on Me a nature just like you?
I laboured day by day
In the same dogged way
That you have tackled household tasks.
   And then,
Remember, child, remember once again
Your own beloveds . . . did you really
   think--
(Those days you toiled to get their meat
   and drink,
And made their clothes, and tried to under-
   stand
Their little ailments)--did you think your
   hand,
Your feeble hand, was keeping them from ill?
I gave them life, and life is more than meat;
Those little limbs, so comely and so sweet.
You can make raiment for them, and are glad,
But can you add

One cubit to their stature? Yet they grow!
Oh, child, hands off! Hands off! And
   leave them so.
I guarded hitherto, I guard them still.

I have let go at last. I have let go.
And, oh, the rest it is, dear God, to know
My dear ones are so safe, for Thou wilt
   keep.
Hands off, at last! Now, I can go to
   sleep.

In Convalescence

Not long ago, I prayed for dying
   grace,
For then I thought to see Thee face to
   face.

And now I ask (Lord, 'tis a weakling's
   cry)
That Thou wilt give me grace to live, not
   die.

Such foolish prayers! I know. Yet
   pray I must.
Lord help me--help me not to see the
   dust!

And not to nag, nor fret because the blind
Hangs crooked, and the curtain sags behind.

But, oh! The kitchen cupboards! What a sight!
'T'will take at least a month to get them right.

And that last cocoa had a smoky taste,
And all the milk has boiled away to waste!

And--no, I resolutely will not think
About the saucepans, nor about the sink.

These light afflictions are but temporal things--
To rise above them, wilt Thou lend me wings?

Then I shall smile when Jane, with towzled hair
(And lumpy gruel!), clatters up the stair.

Homesick

I shut my eyes to rest 'em, just a bit
    ago it seems,
An' back among the Cotswolds I were
    wanderin' in me dreams.
I saw the old grey homestead, with the
    rickyard set around,
An' catched the lowin' of the herd, a
    pleasant, homelike sound.
Then on I went a-singin', through the
    pastures where the sheep
Was lyin' underneath the elms, a-tryin' for
    to sleep.

An' where the stream was tricklin' by, half
    stifled by the grass,
Heaped over thick with buttercups, I saw
    the corncrake pass.
For 'twas Summer, Summer, SUMMER!
    An' the blue forget-me-nots
Wiped out this dusty city and the smoky
    chimbley pots.
I clean forgot My Lady's gown, the
    dazzlin' sights I've seen;
I was back among the Cotswolds, where
    me heart has always been.

Then through the sixteen-acre on I went,
    a stiffish climb,
Right to the bridge, where all our sheep
    comes up at shearin' time.

There was the wild briar roses hangin'
    down so pink an' sweet,
A-droppin' o' their fragrance on the clover
    at my feet
An' here me heart stopped beatin', for
    down by Gatcombe's Wood
My lad was workin' with his team, as only
    my lad could!

"COME BACK!" was what the tricklin' brook
    an' breezes seemed to say.
"'TIS LONESOME ON THE COTSWOLDS NOW THAT
    MARY DREW'S AWAY."

An' back again I'm goin' (for me wages
    has been paid,
An' they're lookin' through the papers for
    another kitchen maid).
Back to the old grey homestead, an' the
    uplands cool an' green,
To my lad among the Cotswolds, where
    me heart has always been!

On Washing Day

"I'm going to gran'ma's for a bit
My mother's got the copper lit;
An' piles of clothes are on the floor,
An' steam comes out the wash-house door;
An' Mrs. Griggs has come, an' she
Is just as cross as she can be.
She's had her lunch, and ate a lot;
I saw her squeeze the coffee-pot.
An' when I helped her make the starch,
She said: 'Now, Miss, you just quick
    march!
What? Touch them soap-suds if you
    durst;
I'll see you in the blue-bag first!'
An' mother dried my frock, an' said:
'Come back in time to go to bed.'
I'm off to gran'ma's, for, you see,
At home, they can't put up with me.

"But down at gran'ma's 'tis so nice.
If gran'ma's making currant-cake,
She'll let me put the ginger spice,
An' grease the tin, an' watch it bake;
An' then she says she thinks it fun
To taste the edges when it's done.

"That's gran'ma's house. Why, hip,
    hooray!
My gran'ma's got a washing day;
For gran'pa's shirts are on the line,

An' stockings, too--six, seven, eight, nine!
She'll let me help her. Yes, she'll tie
Her apron round to keep me dry;
An' on her little stool I'll stand
Up to the wash-tub. 'Twill be grand!
There's no cross Mrs. Griggs to say,
'Young Miss is always in the way.'
An' me and gran'ma will have tea
At dinner-time--just her an' me--
An' eggs, I 'spect, an' treacle rice.
My goodness! Won't it all be nice?

"Gran'ma, I'm come to spend the day,
'Cause mother finds me in the way.
Gran'ma, I'll peg the hankies out;
Gran'ma, I'll stir the starch about;
Gran'ma, I'm come, because, you see,
At home, they can't put up with me."

When Baby Strayed

When Baby strayed, it seemed to
　me,
Sun, moon and stars waned suddenly.

At once, with frenzied haste, my feet
Ran up and down the busy street.

If ever in my life I prayed,

It was the evening Baby strayed.

And yet my great concern was this
(Not dread of losing Baby's kiss,

And Baby's soft small hand in mine,
And Baby's comradeship divine),

'Twas BABY'S terror, BABY'S fears!
Whose hand but mine could dry her
   tears?

I without Baby? In my need
I were a piteous soul indeed.

But piteous far, beyond all other,
A little child without a mother.

And God, in mercy, graciously
Gave my lost darling back to me.

O high and lofty One!
THOU couldst have lived to all eternity
Apart from ME!
In majesty, upon that emerald throne.
Thou, with Thy morning stars,
Thy dawns, with golden bars,
And all the music of the heavenly train.
Possessing all things, what hadst Thou to
   gain
By seeking me?
What was I? . . . and, what am I? . . .
   less than nought.

And yet Thy mercy sought.
Yea, Thou hast set my feet
Upon the way of holiness, and sweet
It is, to seek Thee daily, unafraid . . .

But (this I learnt the night that Baby
 strayed)
Here was Thy chief, Thy great concern
 for me:
My desolate estate, apart from Thee!

If Only ----

If only dinner cooked itself,
And groceries grew upon the shelf;
If children did as they were told,
And never had a cough or cold;
And washed their hands, and wiped their
 boots,
And never tore their Sunday suits,
But always tidied up the floor,
Nor once forgot to shut the door.

If John remembered not to throw
His papers on the ground. And oh!
If he would put his pipes away,
And shake the ashes on the tray
Instead of on the floor close by;
And always spread his towel to dry,

And hung his hat upon the peg,
And never had bones in his leg.

Then, there's another thing. If Jane
Would put the matches back again
Just where she found them, it would be
A save of time to her and me.
And if she never did forget
To put the dustbin out; nor yet
Contrive to gossip with the baker,
Nor need ten thunderbolts to wake her.

Ahem! If wishes all came true,
I don't know what I'd find to do,
Because if no one made a mess
There'd be no need of cleanliness.
And things might work so blissfully,
In time--who knows?--they'd not need
 me!

And this being so, I fancy whether
I'll go on keeping things together.

Listening

His step? Ah, no; 'tis but the rain
That hurtles on the window pane.
Let's draw the curtains close and sit
Beside the fire awhile and knit.
Two purl--two plain. A well-shaped
   sock,
And warm. (I thought I heard a knock,
But 'twas the slam of Jones's door.)
Yes, good Scotch yarn is far before
The fleecy wools--a different thing,
And best for wear. (Was that his ring?)
No. 'Tis the muffin man I see;
We'll have threepennyworth for tea.
Two plain--two purl; that heel is neat.
(I hear his step far down the street.)
Two purl--two plain. The sock can
   wait;
I'll make the tea. (He's at the gate!)

The Dear Folks in Devon

Back in the dear old country 'tis Christ-
 mas, and to-night
I'm thinking of the mistletoe and holly
 berries bright.
The smoke above our chimbley pots I'd
 dearly love to see,
And those dear folks down in Devon,
 how they'll talk and think of me.

Owd Ben'll bring the letters, Christmas
 morn, and if there's one
As comes across from Canada straight
 from their absent son,
My Mother's hands'll tremble, and my
 Dad'll likely say:
"Don't seem like Christmas time no more,
 with our dear lad away."

I can see 'em carve the Christmas beef,
 and Brother Jimmy's wife
Will say her never tasted such, no, not in
 all her life.
And Sister Martha's Christmas pies melt
 in your mouth, 'tis true,
But 'twas Mother made the puddin', as
 mothers always do!

Ah me! If I could just have wings, and
 in the dimsey light
Go stealing up the cobbled path this

lonesome Christmas night,
Lift up the latch with gentle hand--My!
    What a shout there'd be!
From those dear folks down in Devon!
    What a welcomin' for me!

The Reason

"Why shouldest Thou be as a wayfaring man, that turneth aside to tarry for a night?"--Jer. xiv. 8.

Nay, do not get the venison pasty
    out;
I shall not greatly put myself about
Hungry, he may be; yes, and we shall
    spare
Some bread and cheese, 'tis truly whole-
    some fare.
We have to-morrow's dinner still to find;
It's well for you I have a frugal mind.

Not the best bed! No, no. Whatever
    next?
Why with such questionings should I be
    vext?
The man is naught to us; why should
    we care?
The little attic room will do; 'tis bare,
But he'll be gone before to-morrow's light;

He has but come to tarry for a night.

I shall not speak with him. Oh, no, not I,
Lest I should pity overmuch, or buy
Some paltry ware of his. Nay, I'll to
   bed,
And he can sup alone, well warmed and
   fed;
'Tis much to take him in a night like this.
Why should I fret me with concerns of
   his?

Grey morning came, and at the break of
   day
The Man rose up and went upon his way

Two Women

"I beseech Euodias, and beseech Syntyche, that they be of the same mind in the Lord"--Phil. iv. 2,

EUODIAS.

But if Paul heard her tattlings, I am
   sure
He never would expect me to endure.
There is a something in her very face
Antagonistic to the work of grace.
And even when I would speak graciously

Somehow, Syntyche's manner ruffles me.

SYNTYCHE.

No, not for worlds! Euodias has no
    mind;
So slow she is, so spiritually blind.
Her tongue is quite unbridled, yet she
    says
She grieves to see my aggravating ways
Ah, no one but myself knows perfectly
How odious Euodias can be!

EUODIAS.

Yet, "in the Lord." Ah, that's another
    thing!

SYNTYCHE.

Yet, "in the Lord." That alters it in-
    deed.

EUODIAS.

For His sake I'll endure her whispering

SYNTYCHE.

For His sake I'll consent to let her lead.

EUODIAS.

Lord, teach me to forbear; yes, day by
   day.

SYNTYCHE.

Lord, keep me gentle now, and all the
   way.

The Prize Fight

"I am a boxer, who does not inflict blows on the air, but I hit hard and straight at my own body."--1 Cor. ix. 26 (WEYMOUTH'S Translation).

'T'was breakfast time, and outside in
   the street
The factory men went by with hurrying
   feet.
And on the bridge, in dim December light,
The newsboys shouted of the great prize
   fight.
Then, as I dished the bacon, and served
   out
The porridge, all our youngsters gave
   a shout.
The letter-box had clicked, and through
   the din

The Picture News was suddenly pushed in.

John showed the lads the pictures, and
 explained
Just how the fight took place, and what
 was gained
By that slim winner. Then, he looked at me
As I sat, busy, pouring out the tea:
"Your mother is a boxer, rightly styled.
She hits the air sometimes, though," and
 John smiled.
"Yet she fights on." Young Jack, with
 widened eyes
Said: "Dad, how soon will mother get a
 prize?"

We laughed. And yet it set me thinking,
 how
I beat the air, because a neighbour's cow
Munched at our early cabbages, and ate
The lettuce up, and tramped my mignon-
 ette!
And many a time I kicked against the
 pricks
Because the little dog at number six
Disturbed my rest. And then, how cross
 I got
When Jane seemed discontented with her
 lot.
Until poor John in desperation said
He wearied of the theme--and went to
 bed!

And how I vexed myself that day, when he
Brought people unexpectedly for tea,
Because the table-cloth was old and
    stained,
And not a single piece of cake remained.
And how my poor head ached! Because,
    well there!
It uses lots of strength to beat the air!

"I am a boxer!" Here and now I pray
For grace to hit the self-life every day.
And when the old annoyance comes once
    more
And the old temper rises sharp and sore,
I shall hit hard and straight, O Tender-
    Wise,
And read approval in Thy loving eyes.

The Home Lights

"In my father's house!" The words
Bring sweet cadence to my ears.
Wandering thoughts, like homing birds,
Fly all swiftly down the years,
To that wide casement, where I always see
Bright love-lamps leaning out to welcome
    me.

Sweet it was, how sweet to go

To the worn, familiar door.
No need to stand a while, and wait,
Outside the well-remembered gate;
No need to knock;
The easy lock
Turned almost of itself, and so
My spirit was "at home" once more.
And then, within, how good to find
The same cool atmosphere of peace,
Where I, a tired child, might cease
To grieve, or dread,
Or toil for bread.
I could forget
The dreary fret.
The strivings after hopes too high,
I let them every one go by.
The ills of life, the blows unkind,
These fearsome things were left behind.

ENVOY.

  O trembling soul of mine,
  See how God's mercies shine!
  When thou shalt rise,
  And, stripped of earth, shall stand
  Within an Unknown Land;
  Alone, where no familiar thing
  May bring familiar comforting;
  Look up! 'Tis but thy Father's
    House! And, see
  His love-lamps leaning out to welcome
    thee!

To an Old Teapot

Now from the dust of half-forgotten
    things,
You rise to haunt me at the year's Spring-
    cleaning,
And bring to memory dim imaginings
Of mystic meaning.

No old-time potter handled you, I ween,
Nor yet were you of gold or silver molten;
No Derby stamp, nor Worcester, can be
    seen,
Nor Royal Doulton.

You never stood to grace the princely
    board
Of monarchs in some Oriental palace.
Your lid is chipped, your chubby side is
    scored
As if in malice.

I hesitate to say it, but your spout
Is with unhandsome rivets held together--
Mute witnesses of treatment meted out
In regions nether.

O patient sufferer of many bumps!
I ask it gently--shall the dustbin hold
    you?
And will the dust-heap, with its cabbage
    stumps,

At last enfold you?

It ought. And yet with gentle hands I
   place
You with my priceless Delft and Dresden
   china,
For sake of one who loved your homely
   face
In days diviner.

To a Rebellious Daughter

You call authority "a grievous thing."
With careless hands you snap the
   leading string,
And, for a frolic (so it seems to you),
Put off the old love, and put on the new.

For "What does Mother know of love?"
   you say.
"Did her soul ever thrill?
Did little tendernesses ever creep
Into her dreams, and over-ride her will?
Did her eyes shine, or her heart ever leap
As my heart leaps to-day?
I, who am young; who long to try my
   wings!

How should she understand,

She, with her calm cool hand?
She never felt such yearnings? And,
   beside,
It's clear I can't be tied
For ever to my mother's apron strings."

There are Infinities of Knowledge, dear.
And there are mysteries, not yet made
   clear
To you, the Uninitiate. . . . Life's book
Is open, yes; but you may only look
At its first section. Youth
Is part, not all, the truth.
It is impossible that you should see
The end from the beginning perfectly.

You answer: "Even so.
But how can Mother know,
Who meditates upon the price of bacon?
On 'liberties' the charwoman has taken,
And on the laundry's last atrocities?
She knows her cookery book,
And how a joint of English meat should
   look.
But all such things as these
Make up her life. She dwells in tents,
   but I
In a vast temple open to the sky."

Yet, time was, when that Mother stooped
   to learn
The language written in your infant face.
For years she walked your pace,

And none but she interpreted your chatter.
Who else felt interest in such pitter-patter?
Or, weary, joined in all your games with
    zest,
And managed with a minimum of rest?
Now, is it not your turn
To bridge the gulf, to span the gap be-
    tween you?
To-day, before Death's angel over-lean
    you,
Before your chance is gone?
This is worth thinking on.

"Are mothers blameless, then?" Nay,
    dearie, nay.
Nor even tactful, always. Yet there may
Come some grey dawning in the by
    and by,
When, no more brave, nor sure, nor strong,
    you'll cry
Aloud to God, for that despised thing,
The old dear comfort--Mother's apron
    string.

For Mothering!

Up to the Hall, my lady there'll wear
   her satin gown,
For little Miss and Master'll be coming
   down from town.
Oh ay, the childern's coming! The
   CHILDERN did I say?
Of course, they're man and woman grown,
   this many and many a day.
But still, my lady's mouth do smile, and
   squire looks fit to sing,
As Master John and Miss Elaine is coming
   Mothering.

Then down to Farmer Westacott's, there's
   doings fine and grand,
Because young Jake is coming home from
   sea, you understand.
Put into port but yesternight, and when
   he steps ashore,
'Tis coming home the laddie is, to Somer-
   set once more.
And so her's baking spicy cakes, and stir-
   ring raisins in,
To welcome of her only chick, who's
   coming Mothering.

And what of we? And ain't we got no
   childern for to come?
Well, yes! There's Sam and Henery,
   and they'll be coming home.

And Ned is very nigh six foot, and Joe is
 six foot three!
But childern still to my good man, and
 childern still to me!
And all the vi'lets seem to know, and all
 the thrushes sing,
As how our Kate, and Bess and Flo is
 coming Mothering.

Little Fan

When little Fanny came to town, I
 felt as I could sing!
She were the sprackest little maid, the
 sharpest, pertest thing.
Her mother were as proud as punch, and
 as for I--well, there!
I never see sich gert blue eyes, I never
 see sich hair!
"If all the weans in Somerset," says I,
 "was standin' here,
Not one could hold a candle light, 'long-
 side our little dear."

Now FANNY'S little Fan have come! She's
 clingin' round my knees,
She's asking me for sups of tea, and bites
 of bread and cheese.
She's climbing into grandma's bed, she's

    stroking grandma's face.
She's tore my paper into bits and strawed
    it round the place.
"If all the weans in all the world," says
    I, "was standin' here,
Not one could hold a farthin' dip to
    Fanny's little dear!"
For Fanny's little Fanny--oh, she's took
    the heart of me!
'Tis childern's childern is the CROWN of
    humble folk like we!

The Naughty Day

I've had a naughty day to-day.
   I scrunched a biscuit in my hair,
And dipped my feeder in the milk,
   And spread my rusk upon a chair.

When mother put me in my bath,
   I tossed the water all about,
And popped the soap upon my head,
   And threw the sponge and flannel out.

I wouldn't let her put my hand
   Inside the arm-hole of my vest;
I held the sleeve until she said
   I really never SHOULD be dressed.

And while she made the beds, I found
   Her tidy, and took out the hairs;
And then I got the water-can
   And tipped it headlong down the stairs.

I crawled along the kitchen floor,
   And got some coal out of the box,
And drew black pictures on the walls,
   And wiped my fingers on my socks.

Oh, this HAS been a naughty day!
   That's why they've put me off to bed.
"He CAN'T get into mischief there,
   Perhaps we'll have some peace," they
     said.

They put the net across my cot,
   Or else downstairs again I'd creep.
But, see, I'll suck the counterpane
   To PULP before I go to sleep!

To a Little White Bird

Into the world you came, and I was
   dumb,
 Because "God did it," so the wise ones
   said;
I wonder sometimes "Did you really
   come?"

And "Are you truly . . . DEAD?"

Thus you went out--alone and uncaressed;
  O sweet, soft thing, in all your infant
    grace,
I never held you in my arms, nor pressed
  Warm kisses on your face!

But, in the Garden of the Undefiled,
  My soul will claim you . . . you, and
    not another;
I shall hold out my arms, and say "MY
  CHILD!"
And you will call me "MOTHER!"

Because

(PSALM CXVI.)

Because He heard my voice, and
  answered me,
Because He listened, ah, so patiently,
In those dark days, when sorrowful, alone,
I knelt with tears, and prayed Him for a
  stone;
Because He said me "Nay," and then in-
  stead,
Oh, wonderful sweet truth! He gave me
  bread,

Set my heart singing all in sweet accord;
Because of this, I love--I love the Lord!

When He Comes

"When He comes!
 My sweetest 'When'!"
        C. ROSSETTI.

Thus may it be (I thought) at some
    day's close,
Some lilac-haunted eve, when every rose
Breathes forth its incense. May He find
    me there,
In holy leisure, lifting hands of prayer,
In some sweet garden place,
To catch the first dear wonder of His Face!

Or, in my room above,
In silent meditation of His love,
  My soul illumined with a rapture rare.
It would be sweet, if even then, these eyes
Might glimpse Him coming in the East-
    ern skies,
  And be caught up to meet Him in the
    air.

But now! Ah, now, the days
Rush by their hurrying ways!

No longer know I vague imaginings,
For every hour has wings.
Yet my heart watches . . . as I work I
   say,
All simply, to Him: "Come! And if to-day,
Then wilt Thou find me thus: just as I
   am--
Tending my household; stirring goose-
   berry jam;
Or swiftly rinsing tiny vests and hose,
With puzzled forehead patching some one's
   clothes;
Guiding small footsteps, swift to hear, and
   run,
From early dawn till setting of the sun."

And whensoe'er He comes, I'll rise and go,
Yes, all the gladlier that He found me so.

PART II. OUT OF DOORS

Early Spring

Quick through the gates of Fairyland
   The South Wind forced his way.
'Twas his to make the Earth forget
   Her grief of yesterday.
"'Tis mine," cried he, "to bring her joy!"
   And on his lightsome feet
In haste he slung the snowdrop bells,
Pushed past the Fairy sentinels,
   And out with laughter sweet.

Clear flames of Crocus glimmered on
   The shining way he went.
He whispered to the trees strange tales
   Of wondrous sweet intent,
When, suddenly, his witching voice
   With timbre rich and rare,
Rang through the woodlands till it cleft
Earth's silent solitudes, and left
   A Dream of Roses there!

The Witness

The Master of the Garden said;
"Who, now the Earth seems cold
   and dead,
Will by his fearless witnessing
Hold men's hearts for the tardy spring?"

"Not yet. I am but half awake,"
All drowsily the Primrose spake.
And fast the sleeping Daffodils
Had folded up their golden frills.

"Indeed," the frail Anemone
Said softly, "'tis too cold for me."
Wood Hyacinths, all deeply set,
Replied: "No ice has melted yet."

When suddenly, with smile so bright,
Up sprang a Winter Aconite,
And to the Master joyfully
She cried: "I will the witness be."

In Somerset

In Somerset they guide the plough
From early dawn till twilight now.
The good red earth smells sweeter yet,
Behind the plough, in Somerset.
The celandines round last year's mow
Blaze out . . . and with his old-time vow
The South Wind woos the Violet,
In Somerset.

Then, every brimming dyke and trough
Is laughing wide with ripples now,
And oh, 'tis easy to forget
That wintry winds can sigh and sough,
When thrushes chant on every bough
In Somerset!

Song of a Woodland Stream

Silent was I, and so still,
As day followed day.
Imprisoned until
King Frost worked his will.
Held fast like a vice,
In his cold hand of ice,
For fear kept me silent, and lo

He had wrapped me around and about
    with a mantle of snow.

But sudden there spake
One greater than he.
Then my heart was awake,
And my spirit ran free.

At His bidding my bands fell apart, He
    had burst them asunder.
I can feel the swift wind rushing by me,
    once more the old wonder
Of quickening sap stirs my pulses--I
    shout in my gladness,
Forgetting the sadness,
For the Voice of the Lord fills the air!

And forth through the hollow I go, where
    in glad April weather,
The trees of the forest break out into
    singing together.
And here the frail windflowers will cluster,
    with young ferns uncurling,
Where broader and deeper my waters go
    eddying, whirling,
To meet the sweet Spring on her journey
    --His servant to be,
Whose word set me free!

Luggage in Advance

"The Fairies must have come," I
   said,
"For through the moist leaves, brown and
   dead,
The Primroses are pushing up,
And here's a scarlet Fairy-cup.
They must have come, because I see
A single Wood Anemone,
The flower that everybody knows
The Fairies use to scent their clothes.
And hark! The South Wind blowing, fills
The trumpets of the Daffodils.
They MUST have come!"

        Then loud to me
Sang from a budding cherry tree,
A cheerful Thrush . . . "I say! I say!
The Fairy Folk are on their way.
Look out! Look out! Beneath your feet,
Are all their treasures: Sweet! Sweet!
   Sweet!
They could not carry them, you see,
Those caskets crammed with witchery,
So ready for the first Spring dance,
They sent their Luggage in Advance!"

At the Cross Roads

There I halted. Further down the
   hollow
Stood the township, where my errand lay.
Firm my purpose, till a voice cried
   (Follow!
Come this way--I tell you--come this
   way!)

Silence, Thrush! You know I think of
   buying
A Spring-tide hat; my frock is worn and
   old.
So to the shops I go. What's that you're
   crying?
(Here! Come here! And gather primrose
   gold.)
Well, yes. Some day I will; but time is
   going.
I haste to purchase silks and satins fair.
I'm all in rags. (The Lady's Smock is
   showing
Up yonder, in the little coppice there.)

And wood anemones spread out their
   laces;
Each celandine has donned a silken gown;
The violets are lifting shy sweet faces.
(And there's a chiff-chaff, soft, and slim, and
   brown.)

But what about my hat? (The bees are
   humming.)
And my new frock? (The hawthorn's
   budding free!
Sweet! Oh, so sweet!) Well, have your
   way. I'm coming!
And who's to blame for that? (Why, me!
   Me! Me!)

Summer met Me

Summer met me in the glade,
  With a host of fair princesses,
Golden iris, foxgloves staid,
  Sunbeams flecked their gorgeous dresses.
Roses followed in her train,
  Creamy elder-flowers beset me,
Singing, down the scented lane,
  Summer met me!

Summer met me! Harebells rang,
  Honeysuckle clustered near,
As the royal pageant sang
  Songs enchanting to the ear.
Rainy days may come apace,
  Nevermore to grieve or fret me,
Since, in all her radiant grace,
  Summer met me!

The Carrier

"Owd John's got past his work," said
   they,
Last week as ever was--"don't pay
To send by him. He's stoopid, too,
And brings things what won't never do.
We'll send by post, he is that slow.
And that owd hoss of his can't go."

But 'smornin', well, 'twas fun to see
The gentlefolks run after we.
Squire's lady stopped I in the lane,
"Oh," says she, "goin' to town again?
You'll not mind calling into Bings
To fetch my cakes and buns and things?
I've got a party comin' on,
And nought to eat . . . so, DO 'ee, John."

Then, up the street, who should I see,
But old Mam Bessant hail'n' me.
And Doctor's wife, and Mrs. Higgs
Was wantin' vittles for their pigs,
And would I bring some? (Well, what
   nex'?)
And Granny Dunn has broke her specs,
And wants 'em mended up in town,
So would John call and bring 'em down
To-night . . . ? and so the tale goes on,
'Tis, "Sure you will, now DO 'ee, John."

Well, 'tis a hevil wind that blows

Nobody any good; it shows
As owd John haves his uses yet,
Though now and then he do forget.
Gee up, owd gal. When strikes is on,
They're glad of pore owd stoopid John.

The Lad's Love by the Gate

Down in the dear West Country,
    there's a garden where I know
 The Spring is rioting this hour, though
    I am far away--
Where all the glad flower-faces are old
    loves of long ago,
 And each in its accustomed place is
    blossoming to-day.

The lilac drops her amethysts upon the
    mossy wall,
 While in her boughs a cheerful thrush
    is calling to his mate.
Dear breath of mignonette and stocks!
    I love you, know you all.
 And, oh, the fragrant spices from the
    lad's love by the gate!

Kind wind from the West Country, wet
    wind, but scented so,
 That straight from my dear garden

you seem but lately come,
Just tell me of the yellow broom, the
   guelder rose's snow,
  And of the tangled clematis where
   myriad insects hum.

Oh, is there any heartsease left, or any
   rosemary?
  And in their own green solitudes, say,
   do the lilies wait?
I knew it! Gentle wind, but once--
   speak low and tenderly--
  How fares it--tell me truly--with the
   lad's love by the gate?

The Thrush

Across the land came a magic word
  When the earth was bare and
   lonely,
And I sit and sing of the joyous spring,
  For 'twas I who heard, I only!
Then dreams came by, of the gladsome
   days,
  Of many a wayside posy;
For a crocus peeps where the wild rose
   sleeps,
  And the willow wands are rosy!

Oh! the time to be! When the paths
   are green,
  When the primrose-gold is lying
'Neath the hazel spray, where the catkins
   sway,
  And the dear south wind comes sigh-
   ing.

My mate and I, we shall build a nest,
  So snug and warm and cosy,
When the kingcups gleam on the meadow
   stream,
  Where the willow wands are rosy!

In Dorset Dear

In Dorset Dear they're making hay
In just the old West Country way.
With fork and rake and old-time gear
They make the hay in Dorset Dear.
From early morn till twilight grey
They toss and turn and shake the hay.
And all the countryside is gay
With roses on the fallen may,
For 'tis the hay-time of the year
In Dorset Dear.

The loaded waggons wend their way
Across the pasture-lands, and stay

Beside the hedge where foxgloves peer;
And ricks that shall be fashioned here
Will be the sweetest stuff, they say,
In Dorset Dear!

The Flight of the Fairies

There's a rustle in the woodlands,
    and a sighing in the breeze,
For the Little Folk are busy in the bushes
    and the trees;
They are packing up their treasures, every
    one with nimble hand,
Ready for the coming journey back to
    sunny Fairyland.

They have gathered up the jewels from
    their beds of mossy green,
With all the dewy diamonds that summer
    morns have seen;
The silver from the lichen and the
    powdered gold dust, too,
Where the buttercups have flourished and
    the dandelions grew.

They packed away the birdies' songs,
    then, lest we should be sad,
They left the Robin's carol out, to make
    the winter glad;

They packed the fragrance of the flowers,
    then, lest we should forget,
Out of the pearly scented box they
    dropped a Violet.

Then o'er a leafy carpet, by the silent
    woods they came,
Where the golden bracken lingered and
    the maples were aflame.
On the stream the starlight shimmered, o'er
    their wings the moonbeams shone,
Music filtered through the forest--and the
    Little Folk were gone!

The Street Player

The shopping had been tedious, and
    the rain
Came pelting down as she turned home
    again.

The motor-bus swirled past with rush and
    whirr,
Nought but its fumes of petrol left for
    her.

The bloaters in her basket, and the cheese
Malodorously mixed themselves with
    these.

And all seemed wrong. The world was
   drab and grey
As the slow minutes wept themselves
   away.

And then, athwart the noises of the street,
A violin flung out an Irish air.

"I'll take you home again, Kathleen."
   Ah, sweet,
How tender-sweet those lilting phrases
   were!

They soothed away the weariness, and
   brought
Such peace to one worn woman, over-
   wrought,

That she forgot the things which vexed
   her so:
The too outrageous price of calico,

The shop-girl's look of pitying insolence
Because she paused to count the dwindling
   pence.

The player stopped. But the rapt vision
   stayed.
That woman faced life's worries unafraid.

The sugar shortage now had ceased to be
An insurmountable calamity.

Her kingdom was not bacon, no, nor
   butter,
But things more costly still, too rare to
   utter.

And, over chimney-pots, so bare and tall,
The sun set gloriously, after all.

On All Souls' Eve

Oh, the garden ways are lonely!
Winds that bluster, winds that
   shout,
Battle with the strong laburnum,
Toss the sad brown leaves about.
In the gay herbaceous border,
Now a scene of wild disorder,
The last dear hollyhock has flamed his
   crimson glory out.

Yet, upon this night of longing,
Souls are all abroad, they say.
Will they come, the dazzling blossoms,
That were here but yesterday?
Will the ghosts of radiant roses
And my sheltered lily-closes
Hold once more their shattered fragrance
   now November's on her way?

Wallflowers, surely you'll remember,
Pinks, recall it, will you not?
How I loved and watched and tended,
Made this ground a hallowed spot:
Pansies, with the soft meek faces,
Harebells, with a thousand graces:
Dear dead loves, I wait and listen. Tell
    me, have you quite forgot?

HUSH! THEY COME! For down the path-
    way
Steals a fragrance honey-sweet.
Larkspurs, lilies, stocks, and roses,
Hasten now my heart to greet.
Stay, oh, stay! My hands would hold
you . . .
But the arms that would enfold you
Crush the bush of lad's love growing in
    the dusk beside my feet.

The Log Fire

In her last hour of life the tree
Gave up her glorious memories,
Wild scent of wood anemone,
The sapphire blue of April skies.

With faint but ever-strength'ning flame,
The dew-drenched hyacinthine spires
Were lost, as red-gold bracken came,
With maple bathed in living fires.

Grey smoke of ancient clematis
Towards the silver birch inclined,
And deep in thorny fastnesses
The coral bryony entwined.

Then softly through the dusky room
They strayed, fair ghosts of other days,
With breath like early cherry bloom,
With tender eyes and gentle ways.

They glimmered on the sombre walls,
They danced upon the oaken floor,
Till through the loudly silent halls
Joy reigned majestical once more.

Up blazed the fire, and, dazzling clear,
One rapturous Spirit radiant stood.
'Twas you at last! Yes, YOU, my dear.
We two were back in Gatcombe Wood!

God save the King

GOD SAVE OUR GRACIOUS KING. (It
　seems
The Church is full of bygone dreams.)

LONG LIVE OUR NOBLE KING. (My own,
'Tis hard to stand here all alone.)

GOD SAVE THE KING. (But, sweetheart, you
Were always brave to dare and do.)

SEND HIM VICTORIOUS. (For then,
My darling will come home again!)

HAPPY AND GLORIOUS ('Twill be
Like Heaven to him--and what to me?)

LONG TO REIGN OVER US. (My dear!
And we'd been wedded one short year!)

GOD SAVE OUR KING. (And Lord, I pray
Keep MY King safe this very day.)

Forgive us, thou--great England's kingly
　King
That thus do women National Anthems
　sing.

www.bookjungle.com *email: sales@bookjungle.com fax: 630-214-0564 mail: Book Jungle PO Box 2226 Champaign, IL 61825*

The Codes Of Hammurabi And Moses
W. W. Davies

QTY

The discovery of the Hammurabi Code is one of the greatest achievements of archaeology, and is of paramount interest, not only to the student of the Bible, but also to all those interested in ancient history...

Religion   **ISBN:** *1-59462-338-4*   Pages:132
MSRP $12.95

The Theory of Moral Sentiments
Adam Smith

QTY

This work from 1749. contains original theories of conscience amd moral judgment and it is the foundation for systemof morals.

Philosophy   **ISBN:** *1-59462-777-0*   Pages:536
MSRP $19.95

Jessica's First Prayer
Hesba Stretton

QTY

In a screened and secluded corner of one of the many railway-bridges which span the streets of London there could be seen a few years ago, from five o'clock every morning until half past eight, a tidily set-out coffee-stall, consisting of a trestle and board, upon which stood two large tin cans, with a small fire of charcoal burning under each so as to keep the coffee boiling during the early hours of the morning when the work-people were thronging into the city on their way to their daily toil...

Childrens   **ISBN:** *1-59462-373-2*   Pages:84
MSRP $9.95

My Life and Work
Henry Ford

QTY

Henry Ford revolutionized the world with his implementation of mass production for the Model T automobile. Gain valuable business insight into his life and work with his own auto-biography... "We have only started on our development of our country we have not as yet, with all our talk of wonderful progress, done more than scratch the surface. The progress has been wonderful enough but..."

Biographies/ **ISBN:** *1-59462-198-5*   **Pages:300**
MSRP $21.95

The Art of Cross-Examination
Francis Wellman

I presume it is the experience of every author, after his first book is published upon an important subject, to be almost overwhelmed with a wealth of ideas and illustrations which could readily have been included in his book, and which to his own mind, at least, seem to make a second edition inevitable. Such certainly was the case with me; and when the first edition had reached its sixth impression in five months, I rejoiced to learn that it seemed to my publishers that the book had met with a sufficiently favorable reception to justify a second and considerably enlarged edition. ..

QTY

Reference   ISBN: *1-59462-647-2*   Pages: 412   MSRP *$19.95*

On the Duty of Civil Disobedience
Henry David Thoreau

Thoreau wrote his famous essay, On the Duty of Civil Disobedience, as a protest against an unjust but popular war and the immoral but popular institution of slave-owning. He did more than write—he declined to pay his taxes, and was hauled off to gaol in consequence. Who can say how much this refusal of his hastened the end of the war and of slavery?

QTY

Law   ISBN: *1-59462-747-9*   Pages: 48   MSRP *$7.45*

Dream Psychology Psychoanalysis for Beginners
Sigmund Freud

Sigmund Freud, born Sigismund Schlomo Freud (May 6, 1856 - September 23, 1939), was a Jewish-Austrian neurologist and psychiatrist who co-founded the psychoanalytic school of psychology. Freud is best known for his theories of the unconscious mind, especially involving the mechanism of repression; his redefinition of sexual desire as mobile and directed towards a wide variety of objects; and his therapeutic techniques, especially his understanding of transference in the therapeutic relationship and the presumed value of dreams as sources of insight into unconscious desires.

QTY

Psychology   ISBN: *1-59462-905-6*   Pages: 196   MSRP *$15.45*

The Miracle of Right Thought
Orison Swett Marden

Believe with all of your heart that you will do what you were made to do. When the mind has once formed the habit of holding cheerful, happy, prosperous pictures, it will not be easy to form the opposite habit. It does not matter how improbable or how far away this realization may see, or how dark the prospects may be, if we visualize them as best we can, as vividly as possible, hold tenaciously to them and vigorously struggle to attain them, they will gradually become actualized, realized in the life. But a desire, a longing without endeavor, a yearning abandoned or held indifferently will vanish without realization.

QTY

Self Help   ISBN: *1-59462-644-8*   Pages: 360   MSRP *$25.45*

www.bookjungle.com email: sales@bookjungle.com fax: 630-214-0564 mail: Book Jungle PO Box 2226 Champaign, IL 61825

QTY

	Title	ISBN	Price
☐	**The Rosicrucian Cosmo-Conception Mystic Christianity** *by Max Heindel*	ISBN: 1-59462-188-8	$38.95

The Rosicrucian Cosmo-conception is not dogmatic, neither does it appeal to any other authority than the reason of the student. It is: not controversial, but is: sent forth in the, hope that it may help to clear... New Age/Religion Pages 646

☐ **Abandonment To Divine Providence** *by Jean-Pierre de Caussade* ISBN: 1-59462-228-0 $25.95
"The Rev. Jean Pierre de Caussade was one of the most remarkable spiritual writers of the Society of Jesus in France in the 18th Century. His death took place at Toulouse in 1751. His works have gone through many editions and have been republished..." Inspirational/Religion Pages 400

☐ **Mental Chemistry** *by Charles Haanel* ISBN: 1-59462-192-6 $23.95
Mental Chemistry allows the change of material conditions by combining and appropriately utilizing the power of the mind. Much like applied chemistry creates something new and unique out of careful combinations of chemicals the mastery of mental chemistry... New Age Pages 354

☐ **The Letters of Robert Browning and Elizabeth Barret Barrett 1845-1846 vol II** ISBN: 1-59462-193-4 $35.95
by Robert Browning and Elizabeth Barrett Biographies Pages 596

☐ **Gleanings In Genesis (volume I)** *by Arthur W. Pink* ISBN: 1-59462-130-6 $27.45
Appropriately has Genesis been termed "the seed plot of the Bible" for in it we have, in germ form, almost all of the great doctrines which are afterwards fully developed in the books of Scripture which follow... Religion/Inspirational Pages 420

☐ **The Master Key** *by L. W. de Laurence* ISBN: 1-59462-001-6 $30.95
In no branch of human knowledge has there been a more lively increase of the spirit of research during the past few years than in the study of Psychology, Concentration and Mental Discipline. The requests for authentic lessons in Thought Control, Mental Discipline and... New Age/Business Pages 422

☐ **The Lesser Key Of Solomon Goetia** *by L. W. de Laurence* ISBN: 1-59462-092-X $9.95
This translation of the first book of the "Lernegton" which is now for the first time made accessible to students of Talismanic Magic was done, after careful collation and edition, from numerous Ancient Manuscripts in Hebrew, Latin, and French... New Age/Occult Pages 92

☐ **Rubaiyat Of Omar Khayyam** *by Edward Fitzgerald* ISBN: 1-59462-332-5 $13.95
Edward Fitzgerald, whom the world has already learned, in spite of his own efforts to remain within the shadow of anonymity, to look upon as one of the rarest poets of the century, was born at Bredfield, in Suffolk, on the 31st of March, 1809. He was the third son of John Purcell... Music Pages 172

☐ **Ancient Law** *by Henry Maine* ISBN: 1-59462-128-4 $29.95
The chief object of the following pages is to indicate some of the earliest ideas of mankind, as they are reflected in Ancient Law, and to point out the relation of those ideas to modern thought. Religion/History Pages 452

☐ **Far-Away Stories** *by William J. Locke* ISBN: 1-59462-129-2 $19.45
"Good wine needs no bush, but a collection of mixed vintages does. And this book is just such a collection. Some of the stories I do not want to remain buried for ever in the museum files of dead magazine-numbers an author's not unpardonable vanity..." Fiction Pages 272

☐ **Life of David Crockett** *by David Crockett* ISBN: 1-59462-250-7 $27.45
"Colonel David Crockett was one of the most remarkable men of the times in which he lived. Born in humble life, but gifted with a strong will, an indomitable courage, and unremitting perseverance... Biographies/New Age Pages 424

☐ **Lip-Reading** *by Edward Nitchie* ISBN: 1-59462-206-X $25.95
Edward B. Nitchie, founder of the New York School for the Hard of Hearing, now the Nitchie School of Lip-Reading, Inc, wrote "LIP-READING Principles and Practice". The development and perfecting of this meritorious work on lip-reading was an undertaking... How-to Pages 400

☐ **A Handbook of Suggestive Therapeutics, Applied Hypnotism, Psychic Science** ISBN: 1-59462-214-0 $24.95
by Henry Munro Health/New Age/Health/Self-help Pages 376

☐ **A Doll's House: and Two Other Plays** *by Henrik Ibsen* ISBN: 1-59462-112-8 $19.95
Henrik Ibsen created this classic when in revolutionary 1848 Rome. Introducing some striking concepts in playwriting for the realist genre, this play has been studied the world over. Fiction/Classics/Plays 308

☐ **The Light of Asia** *by sir Edwin Arnold* ISBN: 1-59462-204-3 $13.95
In this poetic masterpiece, Edwin Arnold describes the life and teachings of Buddha. The man who was to become known as Buddha to the world was born as Prince Gautama of India but he rejected the worldly riches and abandoned the reigns of power when... Religion/History/Biographies Pages 170

☐ **The Complete Works of Guy de Maupassant** *by Guy de Maupassant* ISBN: 1-59462-157-8 $16.95
"For days and days, nights and nights, I had dreamed of that first kiss which was to consecrate our engagement, and I knew not on what spot I should put my lips..." Fiction/Classics Pages 240

☐ **The Art of Cross-Examination** *by Francis L. Wellman* ISBN: 1-59462-309-0 $26.95
Written by a renowned trial lawyer, Wellman imparts his experience and uses case studies to explain how to use psychology to extract desired information through questioning. How-to/Science/Reference Pages 408

☐ **Answered or Unanswered?** *by Louisa Vaughan* ISBN: 1-59462-248-5 $10.95
Miracles of Faith in China Religion Pages 112

☐ **The Edinburgh Lectures on Mental Science (1909)** *by Thomas* ISBN: 1-59462-008-3 $11.95
This book contains the substance of a course of lectures recently given by the writer in the Queen Street Hall, Edinburgh. Its purpose is to indicate the Natural Principles governing the relation between Mental Action and Material Conditions... New Age/Psychology Pages 148

☐ **Ayesha** *by H. Rider Haggard* ISBN: 1-59462-301-5 $24.95
Verily and indeed it is the unexpected that happens! Probably if there was one person upon the earth from whom the Editor of this, and of a certain previous history, did not expect to hear again... Classics Pages 380

☐ **Ayala's Angel** *by Anthony Trollope* ISBN: 1-59462-352-X $29.95
The two girls were both pretty, but Lucy who was twenty-one who supposed to be simple and comparatively unattractive, whereas Ayala was credited, as her Bombwhat romantic name might show, with poetic charm and a taste for romance. Ayala when her father died was nineteen... Fiction Pages 484

☐ **The American Commonwealth** *by James Bryce* ISBN: 1-59462-286-8 $34.45
An interpretation of American democratic political theory. It examines political mechanics and society from the perspective of Scotsman James Bryce Politics Pages 572

☐ **Stories of the Pilgrims** *by Margaret P. Pumphrey* ISBN: 1-59462-116-0 $17.95
This book explores pilgrims religious oppression in England as well as their escape to Holland and eventual crossing to America on the Mayflower, and their early days in New England... History Pages 268

www.bookjungle.com email: sales@bookjungle.com fax: 630-214-0564 mail: Book Jungle PO Box 2226 Champaign, IL 61825

			QTY
The Fasting Cure *by Sinclair Upton*	ISBN: *1-59462-222-1*	**$13.95**	☐
In the Cosmopolitan Magazine for May, 1910, and in the Contemporary Review (London) for April, 1910, I published an article dealing with my experiences in fasting. I have written a great many magazine articles, but never one which attracted so much attention...		New Age/Self Help/Health Pages 164	
Hebrew Astrology *by Sepharial*	ISBN: *1-59462-308-2*	**$13.45**	☐
In these days of advanced thinking it is a matter of common observation that we have left many of the old landmarks behind and that we are now pressing forward to greater heights and to a wider horizon than that which represented the mind-content of our progenitors...		Astrology Pages 144	
Thought Vibration or The Law of Attraction in the Thought World	ISBN: *1-59462-127-6*	**$12.95**	☐
by William Walker Atkinson		Psychology/Religion Pages 144	
Optimism *by Helen Keller*	ISBN: *1-59462-108-X*	**$15.95**	☐
Helen Keller was blind, deaf, and mute since 19 months old, yet famously learned how to overcome these handicaps, communicate with the world, and spread her lectures promoting optimism. An inspiring read for everyone...		Biographies/Inspirational Pages 84	
Sara Crewe *by Frances Burnett*	ISBN: *1-59462-360-0*	**$9.45**	☐
In the first place, Miss Minchin lived in London. Her home was a large, dull, tall one, in a large, dull square, where all the houses were alike, and all the sparrows were alike, and where all the door-knockers made the same heavy sound...		Childrens/Classic Pages 88	
The Autobiography of Benjamin Franklin *by Benjamin Franklin*	ISBN: *1-59462-135-7*	**$24.95**	☐
The Autobiography of Benjamin Franklin has probably been more extensively read than any other American historical work, and no other book of its kind has had such ups and downs of fortune. Franklin lived for many years in England, where he was agent...		Biographies/History Pages 332	

Name	
Email	
Telephone	
Address	
City, State ZIP	

☐ Credit Card   ☐ Check / Money Order

Credit Card Number	
Expiration Date	
Signature	

Please Mail to: Book Jungle
PO Box 2226
Champaign, IL 61825
or Fax to: 630-214-0564

ORDERING INFORMATION

web: *www.bookjungle.com*
email: *sales@bookjungle.com*
fax: *630-214-0564*
mail: *Book Jungle PO Box 2226 Champaign, IL 61825*
or PayPal *to sales@bookjungle.com*

Please contact us for bulk discounts

DIRECT-ORDER TERMS

**20% Discount if You Order
Two or More Books**
Free Domestic Shipping!
Accepted: Master Card, Visa,
Discover, American Express

www.ingramcontent.com/pod-product-compliance
Lightning Source LLC
Chambersburg PA
CBHW081327040426
42453CB00013B/2325